Quiescence

MUSINGS AGAINST A SETTING SUN

Quiescence

MUSINGS AGAINST A SETTING SUN

VIJAY FAFAT

WALKING STICK PUBLICATION

WALKING STICK PUBLICATION

Copyright ©Vijay Fafat, 2017

ISBN-13: 978-981-11-5679-3

Published by Walking Stick Publication, Singapore

Book concept - Vijay Fafat
Image selection - Vijay Fafat
Book layout - Chandan Crasta

First Printing: October, 2017

"Words dropped from that elegant book
stay uncollected on the floor,
as the barbarians have left
the gentle reader at the gate."

FOREWORD

The image of a flaming sun chasing its own colors as it plunges into an illimitable sea is a frequent allegory, never exhausted. When one reads Longfellow's:

> *"Fiercely the red sun descending*
> *Burned his way along the heaven"* [1]

a myriad metaphors spring to mind; a resplendent Hindu god riding his golden chariot, a thief stealing away hopes, a divine painter profligate with her palette, an extinguishment of desires, a heartless cleaver of wax wings. It brings alive the 19th century paintings of gas lights, cobbled streets and Victorian characters, villages in India bathed in smoke-and-orange lanterns, melancholic and tawdry reflections of light in bays and canals, the flickering vignettes of silhouettes and chiaroscuro. The crimson of the sinking sun strums at the heart as the end of an era, harkening a creeping uncertainty away from the brightness, of the silence of solitude which pervades sad rooms and cobwebbed corners.

The evening is an overflowing vessel of emotions, poised on the edge of melodrama. For the reveler, it promises bottomless goblets of drunken charms and tipsy *soirees*; for the homeless, it is a merciless clutching of pervasive hunger and an impotent future. A recluse experiencing the *weltschmerz* enveloping him on a hill-top watches over the same darkening shroud veiling the world which the courtesans and burglars so celebrate. The act of setting simultaneously promises the poet the budding moon and a long night of feast to the vampires of the psyche.

Little wonder then that our thoughts wander over the range of affairs afflicting them in the witching hour of the twilight, where imagination finds its secret wings and elevates into other realms. The expansive mind coins words, phrases, neologisms in its restlessness; a child learning to express itself, searching for a frisson out of the ordinary. The fleeting rays of the sun inspire much spark inside our questioning self, nudging it to seek the waving, uncertain contours of the unknown.

In the contemplative mood of the grey dusk does the inner mind turn to distant philosophy, wishing for things different and varied; of variations

---

[1] Henry Longfellow, "The Song of Hiawatha"
[2] and ironically reflecting in its own descent the plight of Pegasus plummeting from the sky...

on set practices; of a cooler world with gentler aspirations. Fantasy cavorts with reality in the distortions of the evening shadows. Imagine the moment of equilibrium at the edge of a pond when dusk falls, a droplet of time hanging on to the perfect silence which reigns right before the crickets start chirping and birds flutter out in a flock, swarming across the velvet sky. *That* is the moment which launches the flight of fancy, as it should. Any earlier, and the clarity of vision would preclude phantasmal thoughts; *The Arabian Nights* would not have the same element of thrill and mystery if they were *The Arabian Days*.

The submerging sun teaches much in its fall…

───────────────

The verses here reflect these peregrinations of the ruminating mind. In isolation, they are hesitant thoughts, uncertain of their own meaning and pith. All they request is the reader's immersion in their figurative pond, making the author's craft invisible. They wish not to convey an experience of cleverness or a flash of emotion at an arm's length; their fulfillment lies in their connection with what the reader's pen seeks to write. If the inner voice whispers:

> *The mortal spirit strives*
> *for a decent death in life.*

is it thinking about the Syrian refugees, the country-less Rohingya, or the daily death of a thousand hungers? Is it also cautioning in the same inferring breath?:

> *Mind the abyss between man and humanity;*
> *there sits the dark psyche of the untamed mind.*

Perhaps it is concluding that

> *A hand raised to strike cannot bless…*

I leave all these musings to you, my friend, while I partake some more of the spreading twilight.

Vijay Fafat
Singapore
20 October 2017

Responsibility

In an innocent embrace
of human trace,
give what you hold,
multifold.

Gandhian

At every step,
the soles forgive the feet.

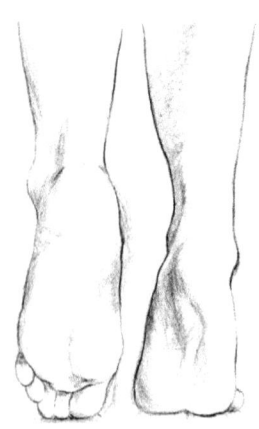

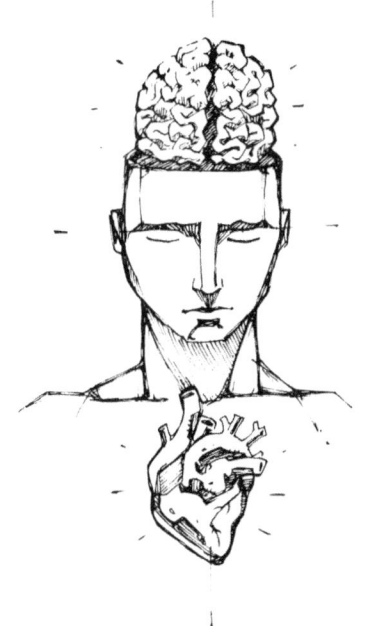

Practical

Suspended in ether somewhere...
All good intentions.

Pitfalls

With care, beware!
Too facile it is
to give tongue to griefs,
and lend ears to flattery.

Mirror

Actions betray
desires unseen.

Solitude

Soliloquy, it speaks to itself,
and recounts the joy of conversation.

A Dark Act

Swing the burning lantern of racial prejudice,
and watch the fearsome dance of shadows ensue.

Detente

Arrived.
A quiverful of arrows
proclaiming peace.

Arsenal

Wield them if you must,
these ancient weapons of choice.
Vicious. Malicious.
The knife. The word.

Fulfilled

Let the arrow of life
get my heart, not back,
and when I fall, let me fall,
face turned to the sky,
in fair blue peace,
and contented sigh...

Man of God

He worships an idle stone
in a consecrated temple,
and kicks a dog - that child -
begging on mean streets...

Destined

Are we not to realize
the ways of our folly?
In war can we not see
the crumbling grit of humanity?

Contentment

Plumb your needs
with measured string.

Holy Man

There is a man of God at the door-steps.
He seeks to know the ways of this world.

Blink

With passive indifference
do the stars shine above,
come famine, peace, or war,
lording over the eternal silence
above our swirling chaos,
which lasts but a moment
on the cosmic horizon.

Precept

Beware the chasm
between Thought
and Act.

No dearth in this world
of actionless sentiment.

Beckoning

Her vision spoke in couplets,
with wine-soaked eyes.
Of distant wonders
were those promises made.

Embossed

Must we be slaves to this...

...this moment of vanity imposed by others?

Storehouse

Unknowingly we squirrel away
nuggets of misinformed prejudice.

Enemy Within

Stand guard on your humility.
Pride strikes with silent vigor….
…unseen.

Chit-chat

What an inordinate amount of time we spend!
Digging holes in the air,
and filling them with endless chatter!

Stop !

Arguments of unreasoning steel
are settled by flowing blood.
Words are not heard
while swords speak.

Expectations

Every destination,
every goal-post,
every milestone
at the other end of a desire
asks but one question
when you reach there:

"Am I everything you had hoped I would be?"

Abandoned

With his convictions discarded,
all that was left
was a small convict...
...a thief raiding his own house...

Poetic

With chutzpah the waiter put up a sign:
"Tipping is not a city in China".

Well, neither is *"Begging"*.

Splashes

Stand clear of the self-righteous man,
for virtue falls without grace...

Mindscape

Some labyrinth lurks
in the shadows of my mind.

Just round that corner
hides the Truth.

If only the courage
to reach that turn
finds me...

Secrets

What stories his shadow tells!
Of places they have darkened….
…Together.

Reposed

Garbed in naked truth,
a conscience at ease.

Care

Tread lightly on fallen leaves.
They are the memories of once-young days...

Relative Grading

Transcend...

...this self-nurtured race without cause...

Admit it !

Recollection most vivid
of things unobtained...

Opportunities

Rue not the paths untaken;
many a fork lies yet ahead...

Regret

Eyes She the creation she wrought,
and weeps the tragedy of a myriad wastelands...

Prerequisite

On bent knees
must we pray for humility...

Pioneer

The winged horse he rides
on bare back with a stare;
takes his mind there
where no one else dares...

Other Shoe

Borrow someone's hunger for a day.
Feel, for once, your humanity within.

Language

What a turn of phrase, this life!
Perhaps another life sentence…

Who would have guessed?

For all the time I was centered
on my inflated "I";
self-important,
self-seeing,
solipsistic...

What surprise!
The world went on,
passing my pride without notice...

Of Superstition

Reason swims in logic.
Mind swims in fantasy.
And Folly...
Oh Folly...
Crumbles in a muddled puddle.

Rhetorical

In the timeless realm,
a question hung in ether;
"Why should swords quiver
and cannons thunder
in the land of Gandhi, Christ and Buddha?"

Answerless to His own creation,
God bowed to Genghis Khan.

Extend

Rise in your spirit.
Reach for the stars...
...Within.

Compassion Scorched

Reams scribbled over the flame and the moth.
Who spares a thought for the burning oil?

Irreversible

What he said
was better left formless,
but wasn't...
...and speech carries swifter than the arrow,
neither paying heed to recall...

Offering

There are lives
which should never have lived,
and some
for which Reckoning should have waited.

Choose!

Paradise

Paint me this picture and take me there,
O Keeper of Palettes!

A lone house
dotted on the distant horizon.
A green palm next to it.
A winding stream.
A bleating goat.
A sleepy cow.
A frisky dog.
A meadow.
Ourselves.

Let's build our Elysium,
all anew...

Matched

When an irresistible force
meets an immovable object,
a treaty of détente is inevitable.

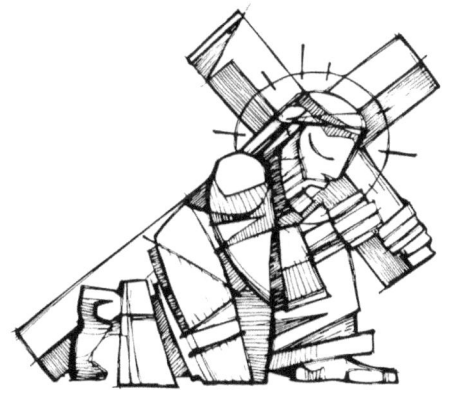

And how!

The carnage!
The slaughter!
The river of flowing shame....

Indeed, God has fallen from His Graces.

Simplify

Shed your preconceptions.
Think with the vocabulary of a child.

Descend

Pay heed to the vertigo.
Put a ladder against your tall ego
and climb down.

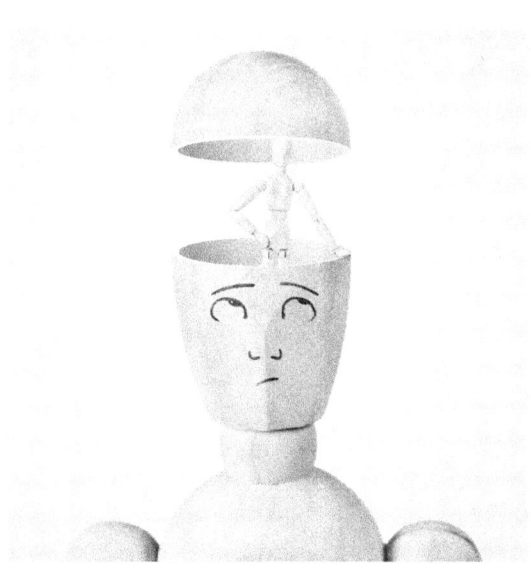

Poisoned Knowledge

Must you open the box of Pandora
just to prove you have found the key?

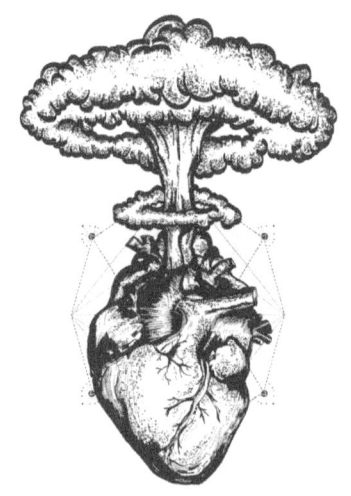

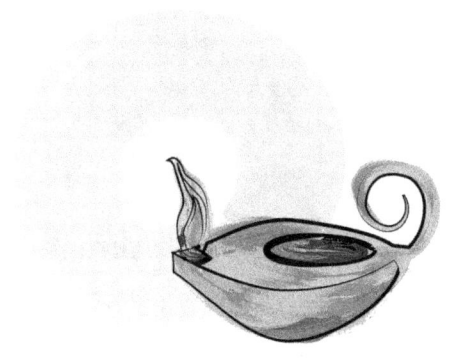

Take stock (before you mock)

O Lamplights mocking the shadows!
Reckon how low your oil runneth…

Reboot

It won't be long before the Almighty decides:
"All of this is not worth the trouble…"

Reflect

Let your pen pause at a comma in thought,
but stop not at the ending dot...

Moderate your assaults !

Is it not enough for the spear to thrust deep?
Must it, of excess, twist?

Watchers

Heavens can only read
what mortals write in blood and folly...

Scarlet Letter

Words, once written,
cannot be erased with more ink.

Ask Yourself

Do you live in terror of the ten commandments?

Unclutter!

Do not worry about the daily additions
and subtractions of the universe.
They will take care of their sums
without your worried input.

Friendless

Do not weep for the stars;
they are well.
Grieve for the darkness
which no one consoles...

Fortune's Way

Disrespect not the doors
which open of their own volition.
No choice then
but Enter.

Molehill

Deliciously tasteless...
the art of pinching the inconsequential,
and inflating it into a fact of life...

Span

A man's ambition dictates
the distance to his horizon.

Binary

A man claims character,
or he claims nothing...

Maturity

A stumbling toddler wants to fly.
Oh men!
And their weapons!

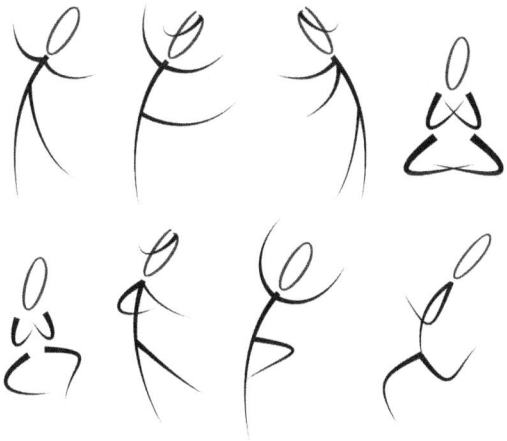

Ignite

The End tugged at the Beginning:
"Start! For I must find my expression!"

Self-reference

The Law of Dichotomy
is either true or not.
There is no other choice.

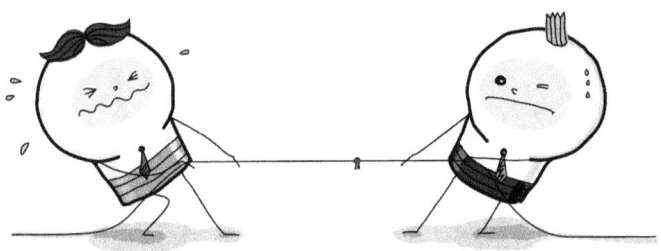

Mythology

The story wrote itself on paper,
and the mythical author was born.
So it is with the universe,
and such is the allegory of God.

Fast Track

In our busy lives,
we have come to expect salvation
through our two-minute God...

Open Mind

The doors of knowledge swing on easy hinges,
if only the mind wills to nudge them gently.

Eh?

Birds of a prayer frock together.

Inward

It suffices to see your reflection
in a single mirror.

Hand-in-Hand

Bravery borrowed from a weapon
often leads to grief of stupidity.

Unravel

In crossing the threshold of adulthood,
beware!
The trailing thread of conscience
often snags at the door-sill...

Unseen

Do not ignore a common brick, passer-by;
the world owes it some gratitude...

Unformed Substance

Gauge the import of emptiness.
Reflect on the form of a keyhole.

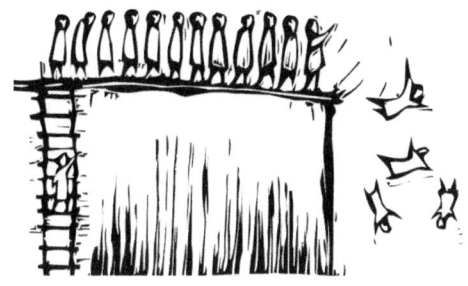

Headlong

"On to the coal mines!",
shouted the charging canary...

Road-signs

The road never speaks to one without wise ears.

Once Bartered . . .

Lay not a claim over mortgaged principles.
They are forfeited in that bankruptcy.

Barely Cleared

In life we unknowingly subscribe
to an insurmountable philosophy of mediocrity...

Twined

The shared conspiracies of their eyes,
they speak in unknown words,
braiding their secret threads
of amorous lies...

Observe

Afore the eyes falls the unnoticed detail.

Religion

What hides in that labyrinth
of bottomless thought
and misguiding reason?

Trust not the warren, O lost soul!
That tangled web...
shackling your humanity...

Decide

A coin flipped
must face up to its fall,
or show its tail;
there is rarely
the middle ground of neutrality.

Preserve

Save a promise
from an infidel's death.

Unwise

The shallow mind stands
on the thin promontory
of narrow thoughts...

Proof

In God we trust..
despite the evidence…

Wisp-ers

A pond of newslessness.
A pebble of boredom.
Waves of necessity.
Rumors!

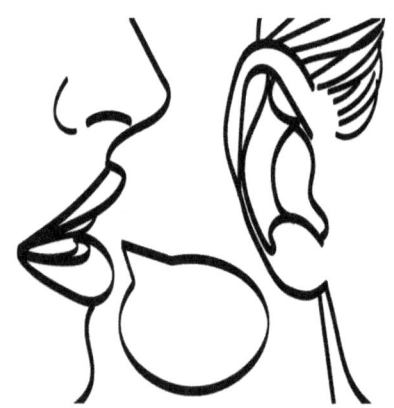

Resonant

Who disturbs his mind
without disturbing
the harmony of the world?

Shades of Nature (Tunnel Vision)

A zebra sees the world
in black and white stripes

Substance

Despite its pretenses,
a flying fish will never be in flight.
For all its modesty,
a caterpillar will.

Steer Clear

Does it ever make sense to say
that the pencil was pencil-thin?
And yet, we revel in tautologies
of intricate, but ultimately
self-similar, trivial thoughts...

Jewel in the Chaff

Ignore the ignorance of others.
Imbibe their tutelage of experience.

Beware

In the fullness of flesh breeds vanity.
With wasted wealth comes the wisdom of ruin.

Lift

Under unturned stones will you find
the opportunities lost.

Lucre's Lure

With a very human lot of desires they started,
these two grains of wheat,
in a serious quest to be grist
for a pair of golden millstones...

Safe Haven

The Good Lord, as our Shepherd,
keeps his silent, ceaseless vigil in the Church.
Of what consequence, if by the myriad,
His cattle slaughtered in the suffering meadow?

Liability

A dagger without its handle
is dangerously useless.

Roooted

Adamant roots
do not notice
the flight of stars...

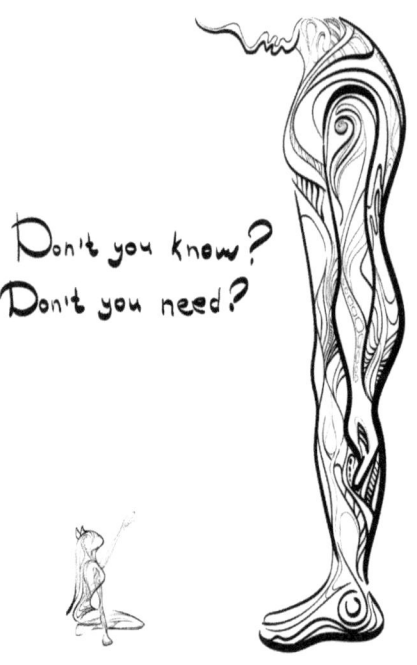

Don't you know?
Don't you need?

En Garde!

Doubts draw the breath out of Reason

Much Ado

A tempest !!!
A squall !!
A gale !
Oh, a gust ...

Rein it !

'tis an art
to silence your tongue
at moments judicious...

Pick a Side

There are shades of valor,
and there are shades of cowardice,
and somewhere between,
is the bright-brush line of Choice...

Oceans Unseen

The eyes wandering over visions...
seeking...
asking...
weeping...
for that one vision,
moved beyond the ken…

Disconnect

The core of hypocrisy:
action divorced from principle...

Adversary

Pugilism is an art,
but utterly wasted on cobwebs.

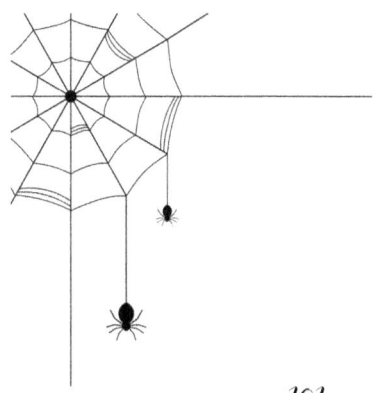

Ipso Facto

Promises made,
betrayals earned.

Open Mind

Knowledge waits on everyone.

Reach.

Fabled Overlord

Over parched lands,
the cruel Keeper of the Skies
forbid the clouds from crying.

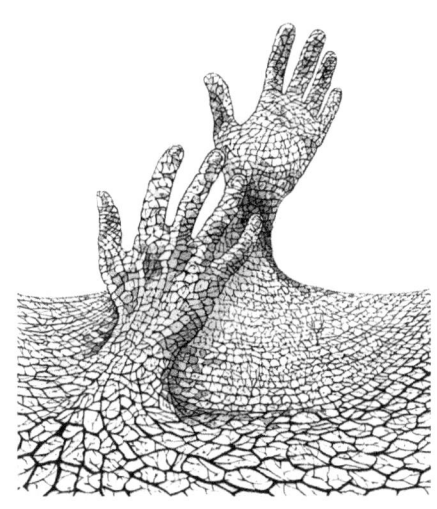

. . . But Some Are More Equal Than Others . . .

On the dance floor,
which was really,
but oh! really really tilted,
the politician tilted his head,
and proclaimed:
"Ahh! A level playing field!"

Scriptures

It may be revealed knowledge,
but you must still understand it on your own.

Asking

Is it a lie without mitigation
if I don't indulge the truth?

A Voter is Born Every Minute (Trump-ed)

In democracy there is...
no protection...
against mass idiocy...

Loin-cloth

He welcomes tatters
who has nothing.

Nature of Things

Fumbles.
Falls.
Inertia.

Recovers.
Redeems.
Free will.

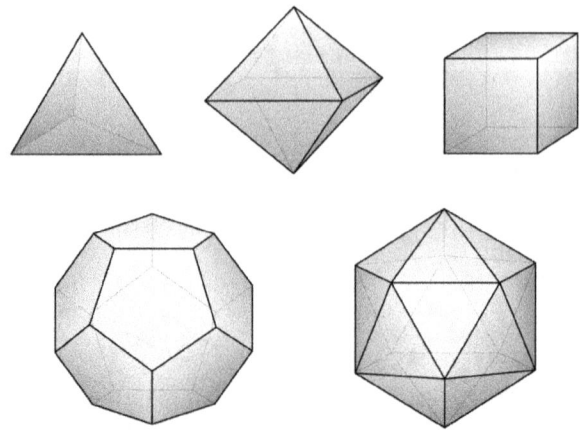

Platonic

Do not underestimate
the elegance of form
against the force of substance;
the form is a pattern of ideas
far more fertile
than the particular instance.

Obsequious

Dilute not
the vapidity of his personality
with false praise...

Facade

Dazzle me not with your radiance;
you blind me.
Leave me just
with the simplicity of your thought.

Shepherded?

Are we slaves to an invisible hand,
or masters of our own will?

Equanimus

Curse not what you understand;
bless not what you don't...

Co-Opt!

A truant wave
escapes the rolling sea
and spreads its joy
across the sand.

Make that wanton-ness yours!

Dip In

A river of unwritten wisdom flows all around us,
if only we paused to notice its gentle gurgle...

Finding Nemo

A quest is like a clap,
needing the hands of two;
the ardent seeker,
and the worthy sought.

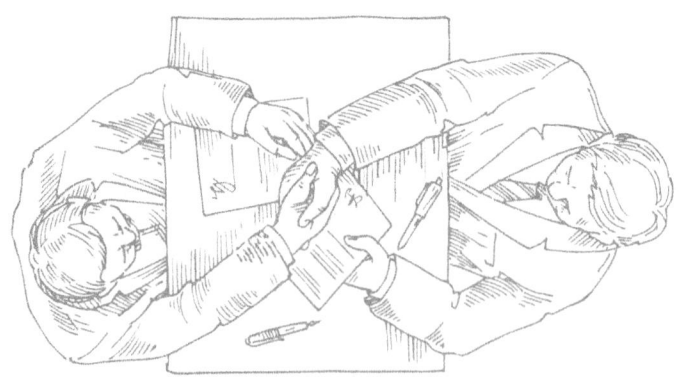

Vacillation

There he stood on the edge of a knife,
a man without beliefs;
afraid of discovering...
either faith,
or faithlessness...
for all the burdens
each brings...

A Good Thing, Too!

Yesterday cleanses itself
of all unpleasantness
with the passage of time,
and morphs itself
into incomplete memories
of pleasant nostalgia.

Dream-field

A dream floated by idly,
searching for the drowsy eye;
or were it for luck,
alight in the world's blindness,
enlightening it anew...

Principles

A dead tree is worth
the trunk on which it once stood.

Elevate

Raise to the zenith
things plebeian...

Think Ahead

Never take a wild bull hostage;
it will make you earn its ransom.

Temptress

Temptation!
She wears the naked robe of shamelessness.

Principia Arcana

All this talk of fire and water, clay and mildew!
Not one whiff of mystery it clears,
and yet, so profound it sounds!

Mask not the Ignorance
in pretty words, my friend!
Lift the veil;
there be hidden principles at stake.

Behind the smile . . .

Do not look at their twinkling joy,
and believe the stars are fine.
They burn.
They burn in their fires of repentance
in the darkness of their voids...

Mis-Addressed

Of what use the shrine
where the deity dwells not?

Icarus

Hold your pride in check;
fly with humility, my friend.
The consuming fire of people's envy
may burn the wax off your wings...

 Rise

Art thou just clay and water,
or a soul of emotions animated?

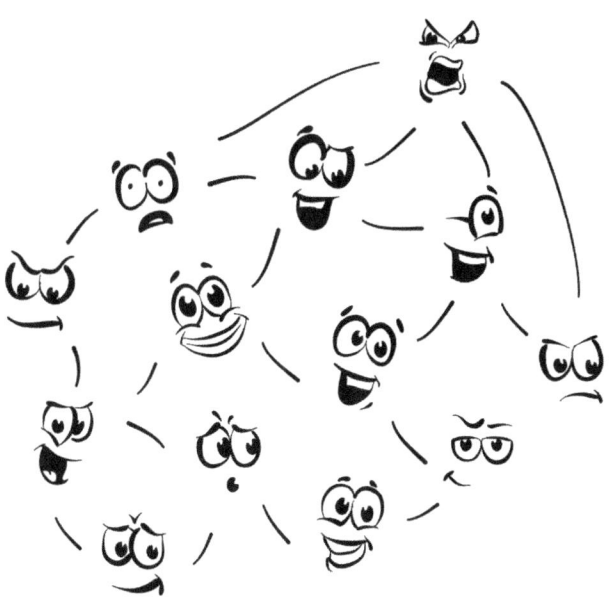

Had at "Hello!"

She was beautiful;
she was kind;
and that, my friend,
was all there was to it.

Determination

We've suffered some troubling times,
Procrastination has caused sorrow.
Let's act! Let's fix it!
Let's start in the earnest tomorrow!

Give it a chance

For an eternity will remain to critique,
what a moment of fancy may create,
if only that moment could deny,
the banality of the critical eye...

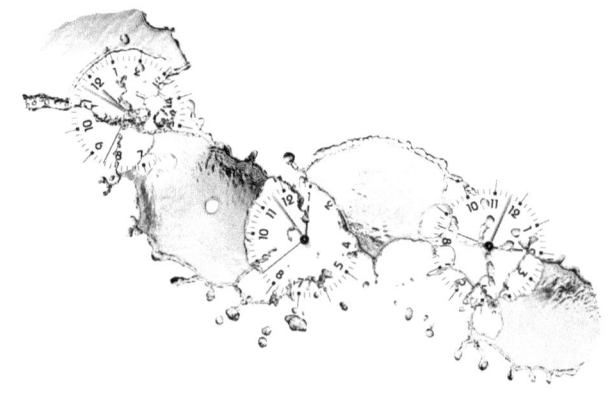

Standing Out

It is a remarkable drop of water
which can maintain its identity
while drowning in an ocean...

Interpretation

Jesus died on the cross,
stilled forever;
it was the Idea of a Savior
which found Resurrection...

Reinvent

Let us remake the world afresh,
wipe out its ugly marks and mistreatments,
and give God an excuse to redeem Herself...

Temerity

Let us strap some wings,
and shake a fist at the angry sky.

Coax

Nurture a song
out of the unruly gong.

The Last Drop

The restless man chases
that last breath of his
for one more moment...
Oh! But just one more moment!
Of restlessness...

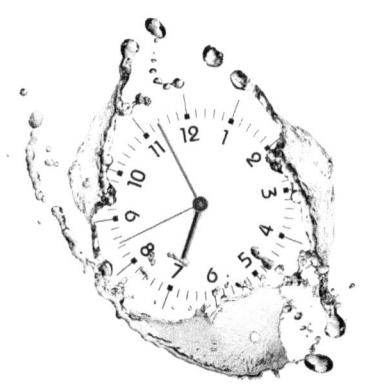

Be Human

To live and not err,
where lies the joy there?

Rectify

We are all illiterate librarians,
tending to unknown books,
reading illegible titles,
floating in a sea of knowledge,
unable to grasp its depth,
and ignorant of its value...

Leader

If the occasion presents itself,
take charge of the timid cavalry.

Co-equals

We attribute to our gods the requisite vices
to measure down to the enlightened man.

Samurai

To fight with borrowed sword,
that is not the way of the warrior...

Err-uctance

When the spirit's unwilling,
errors are unwitting.

Harmonize

Erase this clash
of dissonant consonants.

Subjugation

A blade of grass,
a prayer,
and your submissive will.
What else does the mighty Creator need?

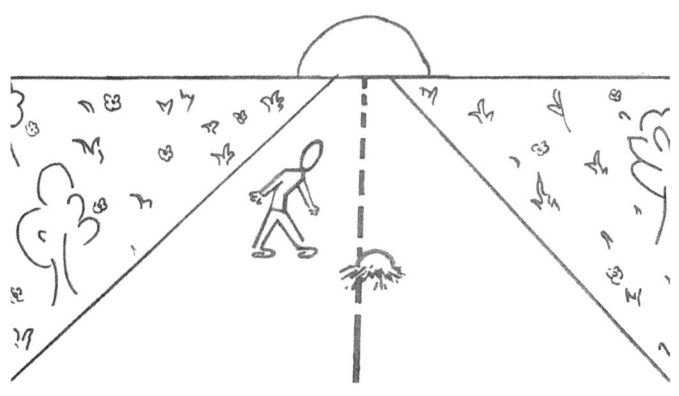

Yesterday . . .

I found a purpose lying on the road,
and made it mine.

Ecrivez !

Write your name on the waves of a breeze,
to be carried forth and far on their vagaries...

Death Becomes Her...

She and life;
goblets of smooth poison.

Soiree

In the sommelier's jar lives the feast
for the unruly spirits of the evening.

Humbling

Why speak in hubris?
Hubris,
which walks on crumbling legs...
Tell. Do tell!
Dost thou have the power,
to reach into the past,
and move a mote of dust?

Conjugal

Virgin canvass.
Amorous paints.
Art!

Consider It!

To beg pardon -
an act which elevates
by its own humility...

Wonder

Think of the reins which rein in
these constellations of stars!

Explore

The by-lanes of life
hide more than a surprise.

Time Enough?

Ask for the gift of age,
or haste.

Struggle

Dueling for my relevance,
my argument with the naught.

Separation Anxiety

Have you ever noticed the sadness of parting
in the spreading waves on the pond?

Recipe

Toss your chosen words into the gambler's tumbler;
swirl them with vigor, as Fates foretold;
unfurl those dice and watch
the tableau of life unfold...

The Holy Man's Truth

In his apotheosis was he robbed of his failures, and adorned with successes unearned...

Drawn . . to her

Fingers of light play on the canvass of her eyes,
painting white lies...of beauty and myth.

Remembrance

Deep from the heart of the goblet,
the wine spoke,
with crystal memory of her,
and drunk as a winter night.

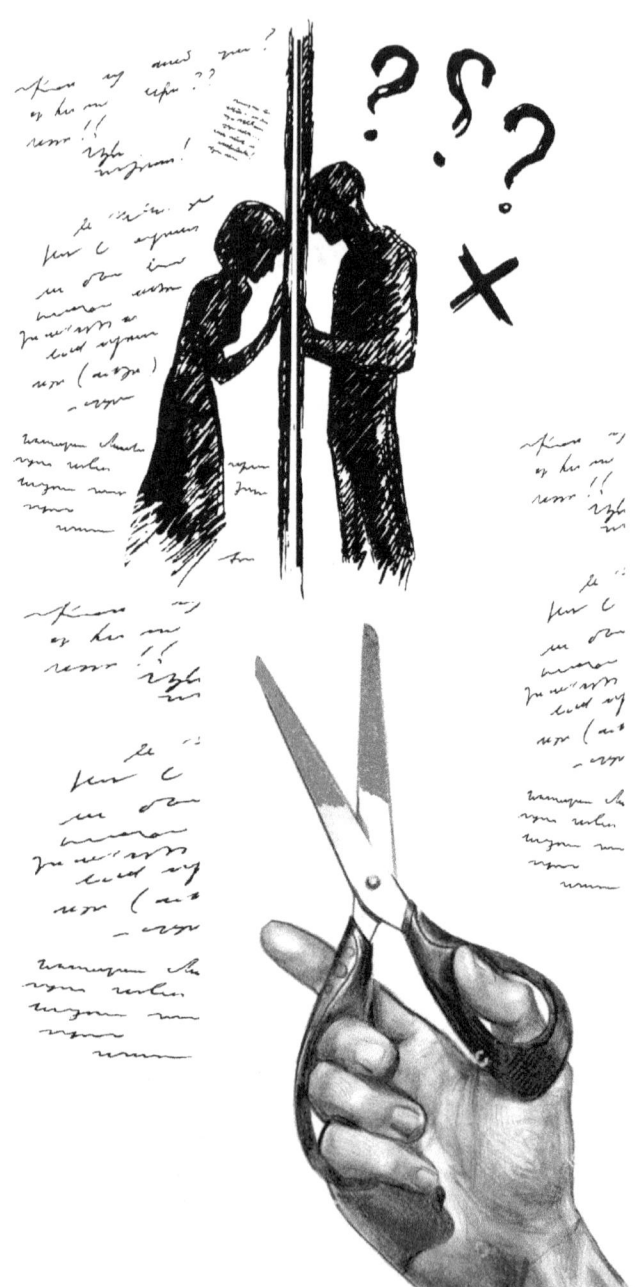

Trust, Or Lack Thereof

In shambles and tatters,
the memories of his lost love;
torn and shredded
by the scissoring blades
of doubt and faith.

Machinations

Throw a few lines on the map.
Divide the people.

Quantum Flux

From the ether we rise
to say a few words
to the cosmic void,
before the voice becomes one
with the eternal silence
once again...

If!

Oh! The pathos and longing
in the blue heart!
"If only THAT had happened!"...

Confidence

Stand tall,
even if alone.

Father's sentiment

Hold my finger and walk, little one!
A lifetime remains to run...

What counts?

It is true that the gods have seen the future,
but it is Men who have written history.

Essence

A river
without its wetness
is not a river,
just a gravel bed.

Expectations

With dejection, as He folded *The Book*,
the Lord said with a sigh:
"Let there be conflagration!",
and all was alight.

Racial Memory

The brown man bears the scars
of white men and dark hearts...

Requiem

Is it pity or disdain one feels
for the lot which befalls Man?
For to suffer Man's fate,
what else is purgatory?

Strategic

Without the retreat of its humble backwash,
the sea would empty itself in its tides.

Feel its Romance!

A moonlit journey,
once begun,
is guided by the stars.

Learn

Even in descent,
a feather keeps its grace.

Relativity

The executioner is never late.
The executioner is always,
and at all times,
too early.

Spare cards

Every man has his favorite sin,
and a sacrificial virtue...

Tangled Relations

'Tis not for a sharp blade to resolve
these disputes of brotherhood.
No sword of Arthur solved
the Gordian knot of kinship...

Ask Dante

Whither the purgatory
for the sins of God?

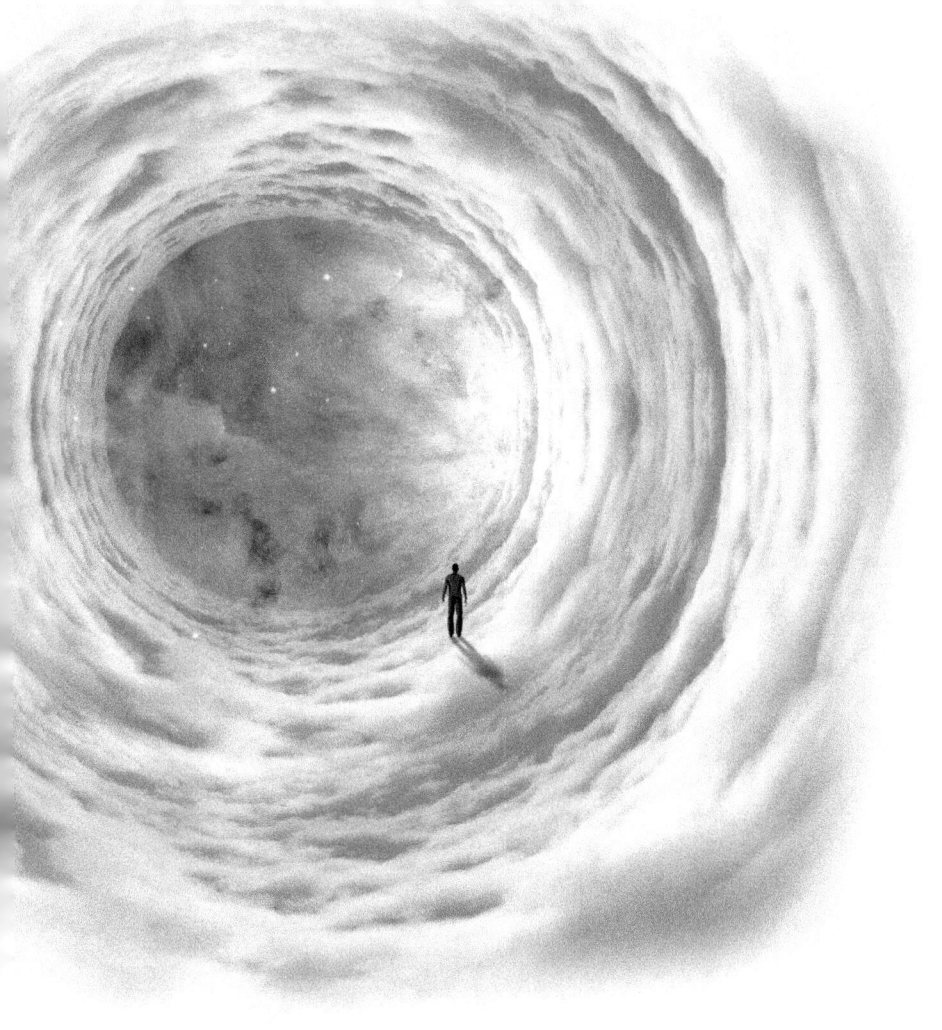

Ontology

Life is a bridge
from oblivion to oblivion,
and we know not
why the bridge exists...